FEAR KNOT

Susan Lindsay

Doire Press

First published in October, 2013

Doire Press
Aille, Inverin
Co. Galway
www.doirepress.com

Cover design & layout: Lisa Frank
Cover image: *Winter Seascape* by Deborah Watkins
Author photo: Susan Lindsay

Printed by Clódóirí CL
Casla, Co. na Gaillimhe

ISBN 978-1-907682-29-2

CONTENTS

No Name

The tao that can be told
is not the eternal Tao.
The name that can be named
is not the eternal Name — Lao-Tzu

Let us then name nothing
— even that is falsifying eternity
an endless no thing
must be something, I feel sure
Stevie Smith would say. But no.

No thing is nothing at all
not a moment in time,
an eternity of timelessness,
though there are many
and I would have it so

turn, then, to darkness
for, as Eliot said,
the darkness shall be light,
and the stillness the dancing.

Taking the Air

Grey-white pyjama bottoms
hang upside down
on the washing-line
two satin pink ribbons dangle.

Warm air, with bursts of sun, imbue.
Bird-chat, wood-pigeon
breeze, buzz of bees.
They'll smell of outdoors, clover.

Satisfy. Evoke rich brown soda bread.
A white damask cloth. Teapot.
Cups. Purple anemones in a glass vase.
Bacon, egg, pudding, sausage, tomato.

A square table under the guest-house window.
Parents, freshly bloused, open shirt-necked.
Hands washed and hair combed to remove
salt, inevitable sand from sandals

left upstairs on the bedside floor to a 'tsk, tsk.'
'Take your hands off the table.' Curiosity
for people — who might be from America, on honeymoon.
Abiding obsession: child arrivals?

Time with father. Mother so much more relaxed.
Children, that did arrive, to play.
Crabs to dissect, shrimps to observe.
Request to carry the basket to resist.

Tears at bedtime. Sheets to throw off, too hot,
wide awake, unable to sleep, legs that wouldn't stay still.
When they came to bed it'd be dark
we'd settle down, be gone — till morning.

Embedded

Rich, isn't it
she stripped the bed
routed, shrivelled
the rooted end

how he
continues
to offend.

Oh Holy Fool

For Tommy Tiernan

You are a comedian
know
we're all spastic —
victim, hero
fool

in a room full of spastic
you know how spastic
it is
to tomfool
with the other guys
as spastic as you

you don't hold back
stand apart
give particular
cogniscence
to amputated limbs

don't distinguish
'offaly man
wo man'

you encounter
another fool
to play around with
get in there
join the laughter

I fear for you. You don't give credence
to the aura
of wellness and sanctity
permeating fools

whose unableness
is hidden
who don't know
what spastic fools
we all are —
conceiving
certain shapes
and conversations
more normal,
less disabled
in foolishness
not seeing
beneath the skin
to the abuser,
lover, hypocrite
carer, upstart
within.

I fear for you.

The foolish,
imagining themselves
not the butt
of your jokes,
have the joke turned
on them.

Punch and Judy
jesters
troubadours
veil their jesting
court fools.

Fear the darkness
Holy Fool
I fear the light.

Form-u-lation

Stone

    y

      broke

         no

      enter

        tain

        me(a)nt

    the twain

      shan't

          meat

       scant

    rhyme

rant —

      reason

treason

trans ex u al

      binary

dys   function

   ex   treme

        unction

             shun

funk

             shun

shrunk   en

        form u lations

ex   tract

    con coctions

        cock tales

hours   of   fun ction   ality

        home to roost

            the belly forms

                 ex…ten...u..at..io.n

        belly to belly —

            cock-tail

            flowers.

The Exhibition II

After a wait
of seventeen years
the public
climb stairs

wooden doors
open
ceremoniously

they enter
a long gallery
tall rectangles
big blank squares

white canvases
greet gawking
eyes
no silvering

to view
bemused expressions
open mouths
blinks, shuffles

one man guffaws
then leaves
shoes click-clackering
on stone

descending
silence
turns to muttering
snorts, rising tones

in the corner
of an ante-room
a last cameo
sized canvas

bottom right
the artist's
name, who

asked to explain
says, 'I grew tired
of seeing

saw through.'

For Gleigh

Michelangelo has had an effect
I'm clearing out the gutters
on the top of a ladder

his David inspiring
steps
after years

hewn muscular form
I longed
to run a palm along
soaked in, absorbed

like a rescued woman
retrieves air
and pure water
to slake thirst —
drop by drop
gulps, glassfuls.

Sean's Health and Safety
warning almost
knocked me off my perch
out-of-the-blue calling
from the road

his offer of help
and your recommendation
that such Michelangelo promptings
are messages best ignored

laughter

the best of neighbours.

Primal

Red
yellow
blue
paint pots
throwing content
against a wall

splashed colour
spreading
        down
across
 dribbling
        along
 grey plaster

earth
  wet red
smeared on body
splattered
  onto surfaces

primitive
   alive.

I Speak to You with Silence

After Czeslaw Milosz

Some commitments cannot be kept
flaw the web their ties undo
when frayed edges rip
fragile filaments
to leave melded blood lines
dangle.

I did my best, we all did.
Although there's always more
to wonder about,
what fears were not faced
what fled from.

It takes courage
to desecrate a sacrament

but fruit with bruised flesh
drops from the tree
to decompose.

Positions of Compromise

What choice does he have?
Will there be complications?
If only she'd stop prattling on.
He likes the curve of skin
just visible beneath her collar
the way her arms rest
on the chair.

Okay, I'll come to the Christening.
Be a pleasure to accompany you.
That skirt fetches short
of her knee. *What? Sorry*
I'm a little distracted.
No, all is going well
at the office.

She looks him over.
Is he really listening?
His attention somewhere else
she wishes she could tell him
how difficult her cousins can be
that she never feels respected
by that side of the family

that he would be
the back-up she wishes for
at family events, that he
would understand.

What planet is she on?
I wouldn't be here
if I didn't like her.
When can I wrap my arms

around her. Immerse myself
get beyond
                words.

Afterwards

he wants to tell her
the unique element
of his latest proposal
unappreciated by colleagues
jump up to show her, on his new laptop
the car he has his eye on now.

Gone
she wants to savour
a slow return.
Longs for him
to hold her still

beyond words she craves
                  silence.

Appearances

All hard assed and sassy
she was in your face
and up your rear
insisting you hear
the urgency of things.
'Move that to the left.'
'Splash paint on the canvas.'
'Turn it upside down
and have another go.'
'There's something missing.'
Thrown over her shoulder
when you thought
she was safely elsewhere.

'Don't take "No" for an answer.'
Rehearsals and re-writes
and lots of neck.
It's an elegant curve
of a neck against the light
pearl white
and her hair thrust into a clasp,
escaped tendril of haste
tracing an ear,
that has you hanging in
for the aftermath.

Pints of Guinness
after the first two
linger in the glass,
her long fingers
tapering
from gesticulation
to a slow tap
to the inside curve

of his elbow
curling,
as she allows
him enfold her

in quiet
moments.

My Love We Must

                    have passed each other by
for I, have caught sight of you
in common place romance
— the small moments of everyday.
In the arms of one I felt sure was mine
but who was not. And in delicious expectation

of hands held after a brush of lips.
In another climate, the sun on rocks
arid sand and dry grass
might have shown us a dark-skinned
chameleon in the shadows
before disappearing down a crevice.

You must take trains across Europe
boat journeys down the Nile —
and into the depths of the Amazon
for I have been beside you there
fire crackling in the black, black night
a chanting dancer.

We may have been star children
may have been made of clay, sung songs
chipped and eroded by polishing,
painted on the walls of caves
seen the sun rise on the cusp of a wave
from the pebbled lakeside shore.

We must have passed each other by
this time around but I don't give up hope
I cling to all we have known and to what is to come.

Maybe, if I close the book we will find each other
between the leaves of fresh covers — another day
another time — possibly, even,

overleaf.

Bloodaxed Human — A Prayer

After Neil Astley, Ed. *

I want to be held by a man who knows
he doesn't have enough seasons
makes dedications to Bashert
lives in the layers when his tribe is scattered.
One who knows he is not done
with changes.

Faced with prejudice
I need word explosives.
I want the intention
        that squeezes through
                a needle's eye
runs fast enough to find father alive.

I want to laugh many times
at the apotheosis of Killer Buns
to be seasoned by Salt and Pepper zest.
Regardless of any man, I dare to hope
    to dwell in the place
    the wind cannot blow down.

** Yehuda Amichai trans. by Chana Bloch, Stanley Kunitz,
Irena Klepfisz, Sharon Olds, Mohja Kahf
Samuel Menashe, IKKU trans. by John Stevens.*

I Have Always Been Afraid of You

sickle sliver of promise
cloud could obscure
reveal too late
the full orb
harvest laid to waste
in dark shadow

the full moon
admits stars.

Life Has a Way

Each tendril
has to have its clasp loosened
plucked from the latticed trellis

predictable diagonals
no longer relied upon

the old growth pulled
out from between yellow grass
stragglers cut back

bright green sprouts
beneath the buds.

Laughter Therapy

Laugh — there is nothing else to do
at times like this
watch the walrus with long tusks
summersault
flap flippers, roll over

the walrus survives
arctic spaces

tusks lengthen
with age
dig deep into ice
in a hole
give grip

it's hilarious
trying not to laugh
adjured, as you are

to *stay still*
on a scanner.

Just Another Accelerated Learning Opportunity (JAL0)

Fearing clarity
enter
confusion

confused
wait
for the mist to clear.

Emblems

She would never have plastic surgery.
Her people believed each wrinkle
in a face honoured history.
She wears the badge of scarred breast with pride
and the straight line where her womb was.
But the grey of her hair wishes to scream
pink and green tendrils in purple.
His blade three cut. 'Bring it on.'
If they gave her chemo, she imagined
she'd have her head henna-tattoed.
Sacredly wrapped to enshrine
                              the *tabu**.

tabu = sacred artefact

Night Mare

Broken promises and dreams
hindered hopes and the rusted
strut remains of a bed frame.
Rubble dumped
over the road.

Whinnying horses, engine throbs.
Half-awake, through the window,
two men in the field
she struggles to wake to confront
rising debris.

Drives, strangely, to meet them
(they were in her neighbourhood).
A soldier on the road
another, beyond.
A training exercise? 'Stop.'

Black hole, straight gun-barrel
focussed above the bridge
of her eyes.
This could be serious.
She should wake up.

Immobile feet
on the clutch, accelerating still.
Maybe she'll die, this way
forget the rubble.
Can,

     she,

        stop.

The Trick Cyclist

wobbles

into joy
hits the high wire

in sadness
crashes
into loneliness

the trick

back on the bicycle
peddle on

dismount to savour
yellow cowslips
on the verge.

Fly-Master

The Dancing Wu Li Masters
harness exuberance.
Source.
As if on broomsticks. Fly.

And I, can catch a glimpse
of incandescent joy
infinite possibilities
unquenchable fire.

Undertow

i

Corporeal fear

  a corpse
     weighted
         in ropes

     below water

heel-dog
   undertow
         against
   current

    faceless

can only
     breathe

    deep

       watch
          seals
           on rocks

             off-shore

       swim to land
    slither
     up-beach

determine
    to leave fins
  behind
    — by tides turn
  surrender

      can't undo

knot
 untangle
   umbilical
  chords
    anchored

  to sea

 bed

ii

the caul

    a wrapped

        shawl

      lure

       tug

       she trails

         seaweed,

        a seal

       skin

     sings

    her

     seal

       s
        o
         n
          g

iii

skelfed
        caul
           shroud

   ensures

     she won't drown

shedded fish tale

        lands her

— salted nostrils

     shell-sound earful

      tides turning

        her womb

the moon,

       dances

          veins,

      plays

    shadows

     while

       earth

        clays

       bones

iv

beached

    she lies still

  in time

     air seeps
        through nostrils
    chest rises
         sucks

      a gentle ebb and flow

      light ripples

      airways

     until
        a wave's sigh

     spreads contagion

kickstarts

      desire

     stirrings

       twitches feet

        tweaks knees

      lifts her head

fuels body

        to rise

on all fours

       drag

         through sand

     upright

     sit

   among dunes

  test strength

    torso

     the possibility

      of

      loping

     legs.

Winter 2010

Flying saucers of slabs
over a river of frozen
in Lady Gregory's woods
ice, where the turlough rose
leaving layers of itself
in frozen suspension.

The setting sun
illumined sections
white, grey, luminous,
opaque.

Pink-tinged shadows played
stick-figure patterns
among tree trunks, black and brown
rooted, uprooted
and distant green.

Bail Out

I've been away
the snow has come
already thick layers of ice
threaten hibernating wildlife

the plastic coated white
leather football
placed in the pond
to prevent disaster

is iced in. Last year
twenty small frogs
were scooped from their frozen coffin
to graves on earth

kettle after kettle of boiling water
fail to float
the rescue plan
footprints crunch across snow

a further torrent of steaming liquid
dents the ice
reveals a submerged frog
eyeballing hope

a further trudge
obsessing, scald frozen flesh
or melt sufficient space
for oxygen?

The wretched reptile moves
kettle and handler wobble
freed, the frog dives
the next morning

is found dead
frozen
beneath a second
plan for liquidity.

The Glory of Rubble

The possibility of unfinished houses
concrete block.
No prim finish cover
for the hazards
of fire, cracks
and shaky foundations.
Monuments.

These estates replace
dwellings left behind
former generation, degenerate
weeds in the roof, daffodils
in tumbled gardens
stone piles beside broken shed walls.

Orange corrugated iron
patchy, twisted,
a dangling drain pipe
water butt drips.

Clustered stone crumbles
of lost villages.
Leave them alone.

Nettles, the twisted iron bedsteads
mildewed mattresses, wisps of horse-hair
grey button flowers.

The rusty range and chair
with a broken leg.

Residue
its own pleasure
hummocks of grass strewn

with broken brown glass
the remains of a blue bottle.

There are no happy endings
but buttercups flourish here
and dandelions.

There's a robin on a stone
a blackbird's song.

Spiders weave their webs in peace
walls with holes in the windows
and the hanging door
with rusted clasp
still provide the shelter
of a dry space
for a tramp who will never visit.

Cows and pigs
better off where they are.

Despair
scrubbed surfaces
in tidy kitchens elsewhere.

One White House or Another

One kid under each arm
she brings them in.
The nanny follows
in pelting rain.

That morning we had dug
our spades hacking to cut roots
and shovelling earth
to bury the kid

taken by caesarean
in open yard surgery
from a nanny
not known to be pregnant.

She wasn't out of danger
but the bran mash
and homeopathic remedy
Irma Van Baalen gave her,

the goat book
suggestion that poison
might be mitigated that way,
gave hope. She milked her.

Three women kept
watch in the tiny shed
drinking brandy by candlelight
long after the vet left

two of them had begun
Caherholly cheese. First

in Wexford then Westport.
Irma told Barbara she'd heard

the current proprietors
provided a recent round
for the Taoiseach
to bring to the White House.

Bogged in Portlaoise

Body removed
to the care of
the Keeper of Antiquities
at the National Museum.

Legs protruding
from the leather bag
body crouched within.

Buried or sacrificed
for ritual purposes
characteristic of
the Bronze Age.

Conflagration — Death — The End

Smouldering remains
black twisted metal
squashed window frames
occasional streaks of under-paint
orange, turquoise, green
              smoked residue.

A wasteland of memories,
nostalgia, family memorabilia
times when relationships
meant something else.
Attachment — a blinding
umbilical chord
binding.
Blinkers, reins
a carriage on course
to an inevitable destination
no-one knows is destructible.

That's all over
black burning waste
occasional smoke plumes
puddles of water
the ironic sparkle of daylight
on droplets, spills
from tips shifted
by a blast of cold air.
Reminders of jets, hosed
to douse the fuming
furnace, plastic, oil tank
flames.

This is the end.
No Phoenix in these ashes.

Such possibility as there is
resides in that
        categorical certainty.

Mother

Encase me in strips
of gluey paper.
A pâpier machée
tomb in two halves,
appliqued images veneered on black.
Alternative masks strewn around.
No. Wrap me tightly in plastered bandages
tighter yet — until I cannot breathe.

Put an end to bodyless
encompass me — so tightly wound
in swaddling clothes I feel alive, secure
at body's end. Mummify me,
I'm a Mummy already,
till the muddied cloths no longer know
whose end they serve; the body's skin
decayed and taken
or, the absorbing earth.

I find it hard to believe in an infinity
of bliss. But even if
a spirit is set free, extinguish me.
I'll be extinct encased in mud
clay's texture, crumble to increase.

A Fallow Field

Stubby cropped grass and horse-manure.
Final fertile strands
harvested. Mud remains
occasional tufted stalks

seem sterile now, unloved
trampled turfs compacted.
There's nothing much to observe
the desultory pecking of a lone crow

a robin in the hedgerow
not gone beyond hope
the worms, though, are secure.
Tattered coat tails

that once flapped on the straw skeleton
discarded in the bin,
unworthy, even, of re-cycling
going to ground — await a carrier.

Hard to believe anything
can grow here again.

There

From the Asylum of the ordinary
visit the hospital for the insane
who see ordinary
for what it is
medicate themselves
seek treatment
for having gone over the edge
of truth
one step further
than could be borne
too much reality
can make you mad
delusional
is much more
healthy.
The white rabbit
is not going anywhere
he doesn't appear
here.

Fringe Exhibit

Wool, wood,
a wrapped cocoon
suspended
on a string
strung out

across a room

I know there's a butterfly
with broken wing
crumpled
somewhere

within.

Twilight

And when,
  the dark lady dances
  and the blue smoke swathes
  sandwiched between Havana cigars
  and breakwater waves

  align on the gable end
  rose pink hue
  tingeing
  ephemeral blue

the sandstone brick buildings
mellowed rose
mullioned windows
wink at starlings
the clouds
of dark jet plume
leave messages
like Buddhist sand paintings

the silent dark menace
wood-scented comfort
of sirated trunks
branch pine and cones

over-hanging a driveway
fantailed pigeons
cooing
late arrival

then,
  the sapphire-nosed diamond
  steel
    flexed
  rapier
    vibrates
   distorting
      reflections.

In the Darkness

of the asylum
she made pâpier machée beads
from crushed paper
the stickiness satisfying,
her fingers immersed in glue
smoothing torn squares
in layers on the surface.

When the occupational therapist
spent the last of her budget
on metallic paint and a volunteer
donated gold she found light
could create something
beautiful.

Austerity

Red shawls
on the Masai hunter,
his apprentice.

Staffs and loin cloths,
bare feet shod
in open leather soles,

they walk for weeks
search for the antelope
prey to lions
whose first bites
leave blood tracks these
last Grassland Masters

seek out and follow
for days. Remaining
in sight.

'They think
we know nothing,'
the men whisper, laugh

at their own trackers —
a BBC film crew
health and safety fears.

Faced down by Masai intent
fifteen lions mauling
an antelope carcass

slink back
triggered to spring,
a circle of eyes watch,

as the hunters carve
off a leg, sling it
over shoulders

walk on.

Making Headway

A woman at the helm
steadies the tiller
he is the mast, sails
catch wind
billow in light breeze
reeled in
taut
they skim the waves

about turn
jibe
take a fresh tack.

An End in Sight

The walls of the
Red Sea
roll back

open a way

umbilical cords
anchored to the ocean floor
cauled to land

shroud life's lure
protect life itself
inhibit

then, shrivel
die.

Grappling hooks
grace
a line
balls in colour collage
pomegranate seeds
remind

a new cord
umbilically struck
anchored

secures
promised land.

Dried Feathers on Bone

Gather
on a wing and a prayer
meaningless corn
a silent rattle.

A closed book
is not the word.
In dialogue, light.
Reluctant listeners imbibe,
engage, reach out in supplication
to break earth open.

A St. Brigid's cross weave
of faithful action
roots seed
to find voice
in the dark, sing
to green
absorbing light.

These yoga
postures
— the irregular
pattern of branches
pared back,
propagate
sap

spiralling
flight.

Isabelle Atkins

i

buried her privates
in a leather suitcase
underneath the lavender.

Took the last bus
to she knew not where
with a Ryanair fit
roll-it, a traveller's
rucksack zipped
inside it.

So don't waste your time
calling at her door
she doesn't live there
any more.

When the post piled up
the woman at the postal office
called the Guards
to peer in windows

nothing seemed amiss
she didn't leave a smell
or anything otherwise
untoward, and with nowhere

to forward the letters
they were returned
to sender with the words
'Isabelle Atkins no longer
lives at this address'.

A facsimile was spotted
among the greater crested grebe
where they hang about
and once, it was reported

a woman matching her description
had crossed a fjord in Finland.
It entered someone's mind to wonder
was she heading for the frozen-over
parts of the Artic. Could she be found

among the puffin. Was she: wintering
at sea, an ocean clown bird
running across the water's surface
to take to air. Absurd.

They learned
not to wonder. Confused
pigeons in the loft, ruffled
went astray and didn't make it home
in record time. Fanciers focussed

on soothing coos
and feathers, smoothed,
flapped with vigour
until they aptly beat the requisite
number of strokes to the minute

winged it on air
in winning time
and everyone could breathe
again.

She wasn't in thin air though
she wasn't there at all
her facsimile didn't take her case
to the great tribunal in the sky.
Dear me, no.

She took the tube, the City Line
to dine and wine, dissemble
on the tricky question
of home truth.

Isabelle Atkins

ii

visited the Houses of Parliament
barged her way downriver on the Thames
took a trip to Maidenhead
without a virginal thought in mind

quite the opposite. She was attracted
to bald men or those
going thin on top, liked
their serious, or slightly bewildered air

the slight stoop of shoulders
as they stood in queues
carrying wire shopping baskets
filled with vegetables and meals for one.

They put a dart
in a heart barely beating
a quick flutter, fledgling wings
bestirred a sense of fellow feeling

and something else,
admiration. She liked the look
of their resilience
was in awe

of women too, the stalwart
crew who battle
smiling and laughing
in the face of adversity

although, the grim determination
of steely others brought a grin
to her face

their dour countenances, relentless
unwillingness to engage for a moment
in pleasantries or collusion
with mass self-deception, or optimism
pleased her — brought a thread

of mirth as she viewed
the daily insanity
people going about their business
catching the same train

to the same destination and disembarking
seriously intent on the business
of purchasing the same coffee as yesterday
before purposefully striding

to revolving doors discharging
them to duties they'd be lost without
she watched them tap laptops
preferred those who ended the daily

commute with an intermittent
chew on the end of a writing implement
as they pondered the crossword clues
of The Guardian or Times or puzzled

suduko, computing lines
of meaningless digits to strengthen
their minds in readiness
for the long haul they hoped was ahead.

Isabelle Atkins
was discovering new meaning in death
she wondered if they knew —
the men she admired

and the slowed down populace
how attractive they are
that her glance was admiring.
She saw them as heroes

wondered had the images of *Hello*
magazine and smartphone
on-line pictures of friends
in star-like poses blinded them

to the possibilities
of their own character, visible
in curved bones
story lines on visages

enduring wisdom earned.
She'd always seen
beauty in bare branches
on the winter skyline.

Hindsight showed her
how stolen moments
became the memories
of note

bleached highlights
brought new ways
of sucking on bones
to get to the marrow.

ACKNOWLEDGEMENTS

Acknowledgements are due to the following publications in which versions of these poems first appeared: 'My Love We Must' appeared in *Crannóg* (Summer, 2013); 'The Exhibition II' appeared in *Skylight 47* (January, 2013); 'Form-u-lation' appeared in *The Faber Academy Anthology* (Dublin, 2010); and 'Bail Out' appeared in *Mosaic: Skylight Poets Anthology* (2011).

'Dried Feather on Bones' was informed by first participant contributions to the 2013 course *Having the Conversation — About Faith* in Killeenaran: Fiona, Kay, Sue, Esther-Mary, Gordon, Margaret, Cilian and Mari. The author alone carries responsibility for the overall poem, its tone and content.

The author also wants to thank Kevin Higgins and fellow members of Skylight Poets for their help.

The quoted lines from The Tao Te Ching used in ·the poem 'No Name' are taken from the translation by Stephen Mitchell, *Tao Te Ching* (1988) in the Kyle Cathie Ltd., 2002 edition. In the same poem, the (broken) line from T. S. Eliot is from 'East Coker III'.

Susan Lindsay was born in 1950 and graduated from Trinity College, Dublin in 1975. She followed a career in psychotherapy, facilitation and as a consultant to organisations for thirty years. Retired from psychotherapy, she is drawing on her former experience to write and facilitate workshops, as well as acting as a co-editor of *Skylight 47,* a biannual poetry paper launched in association with the tenth anniversary of Over the Edge Literary Events. In 2011 she was invited to read for Poetry Ireland's Poetry Introduction Series. *Whispering the Secrets,* her debut collection of poetry, was published in 2011 by Doire Press.